I0467390

Adult Coloring Book
Flower Designs
Stress Relief and Relaxation

by Amanda Davenport

ISBN-13: 978-1519422927

ISBN-10: 151942292X

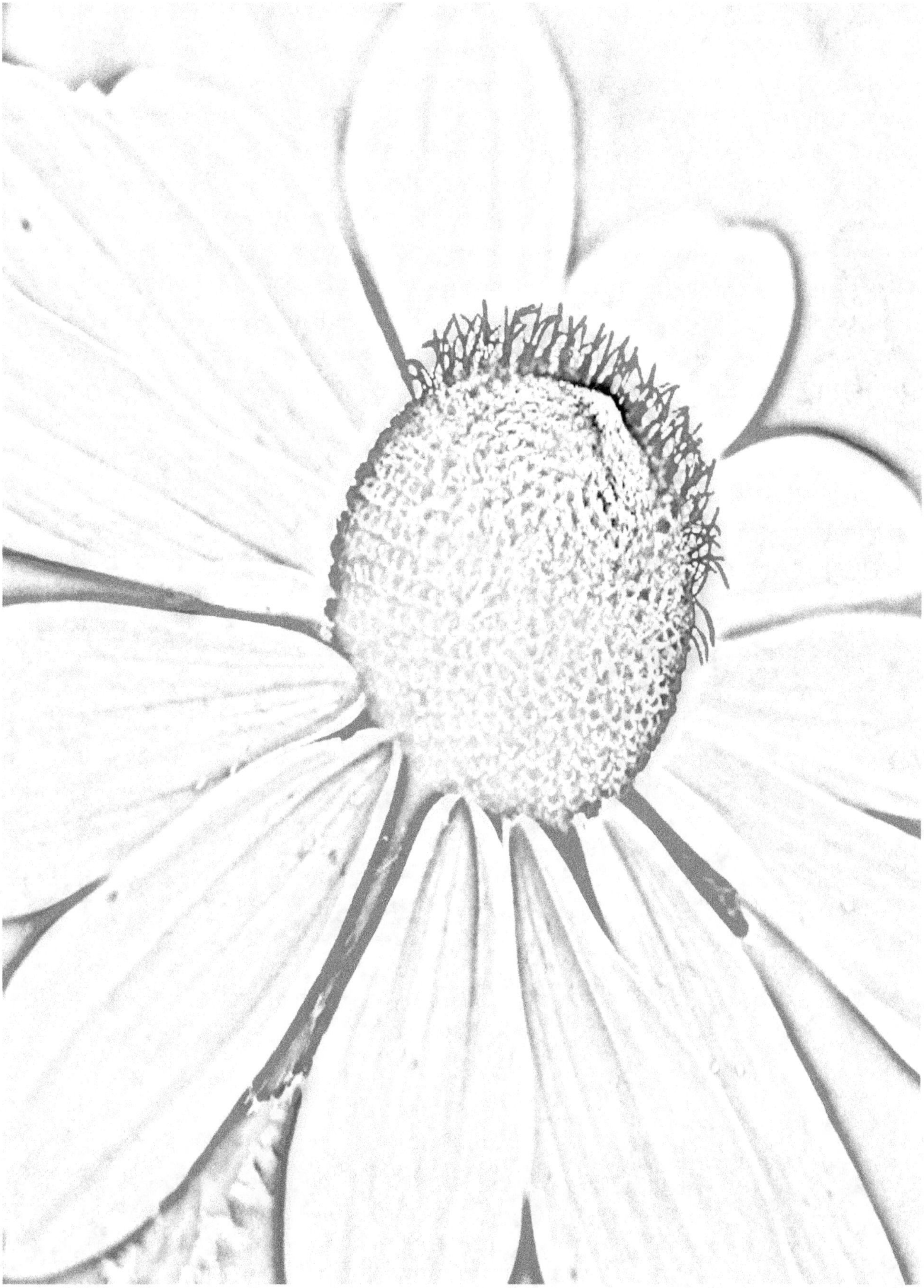

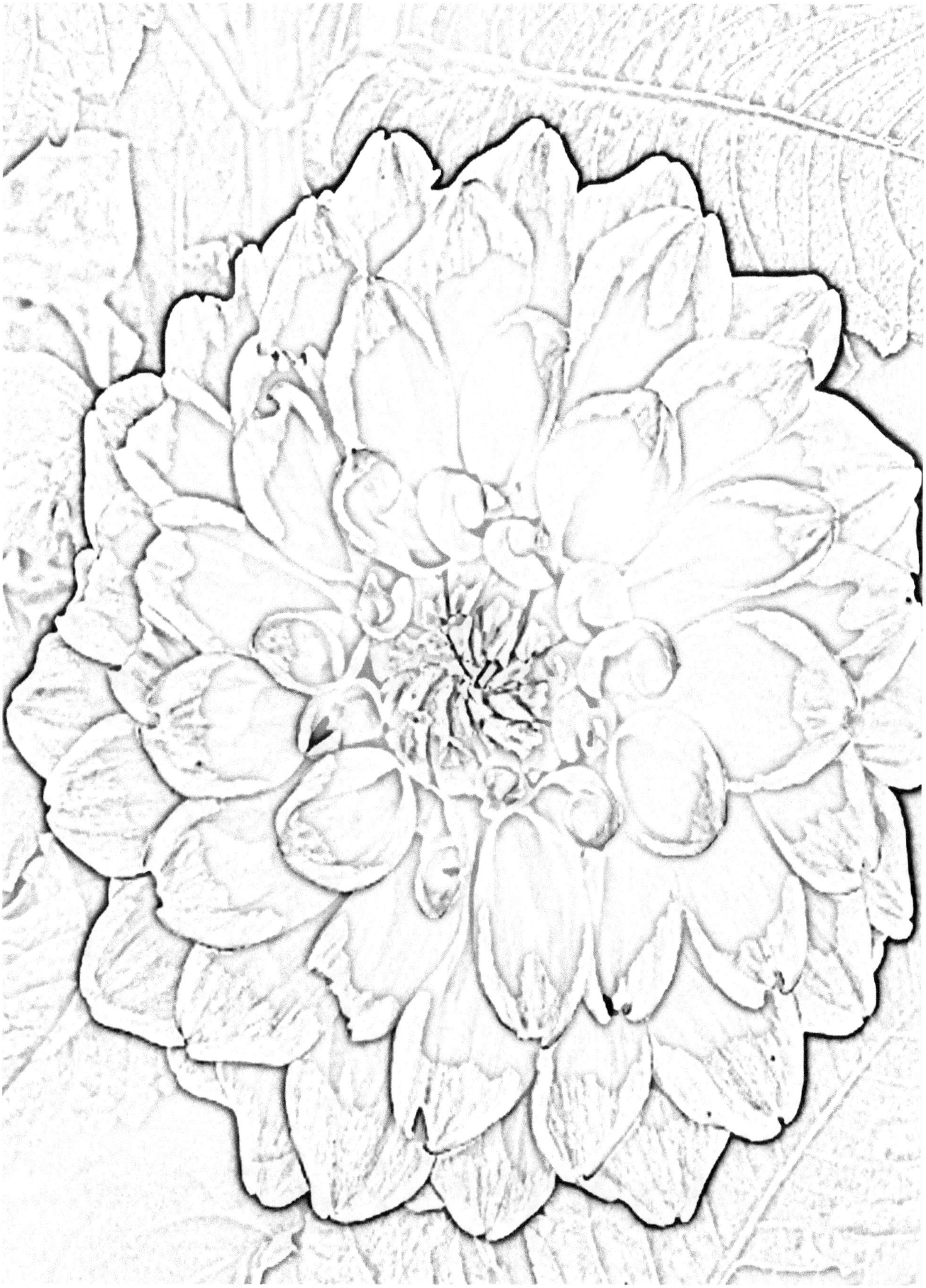

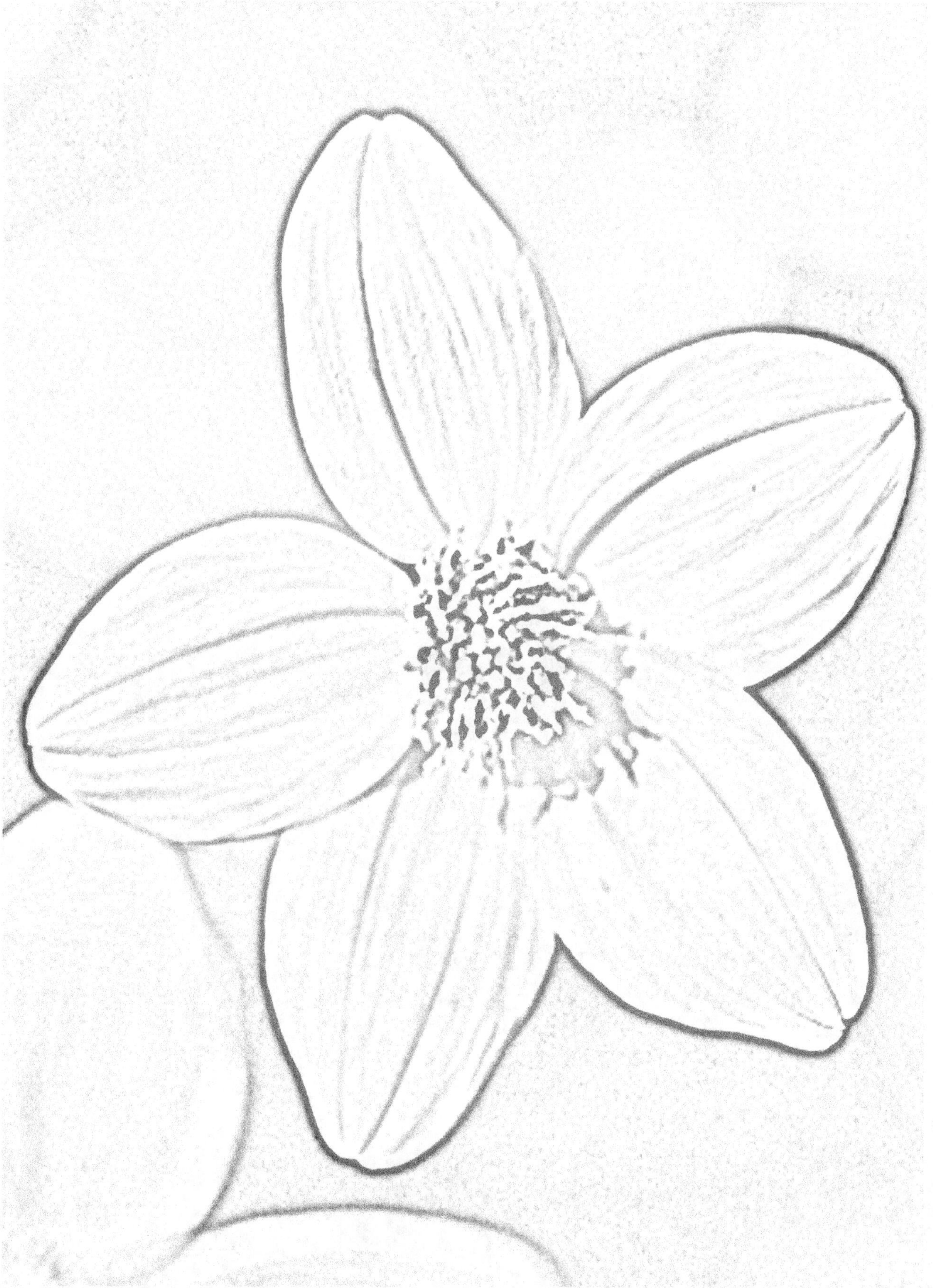

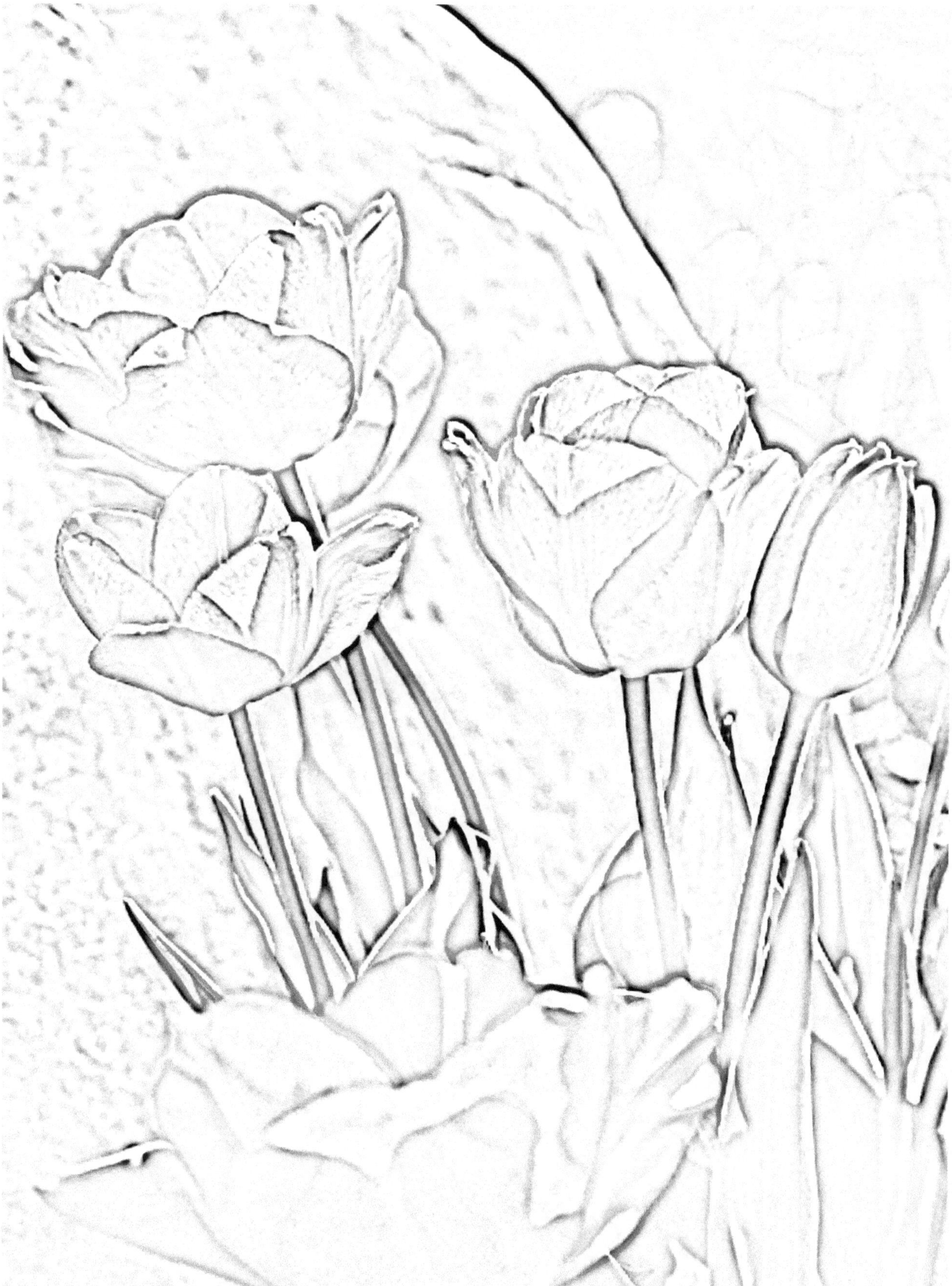

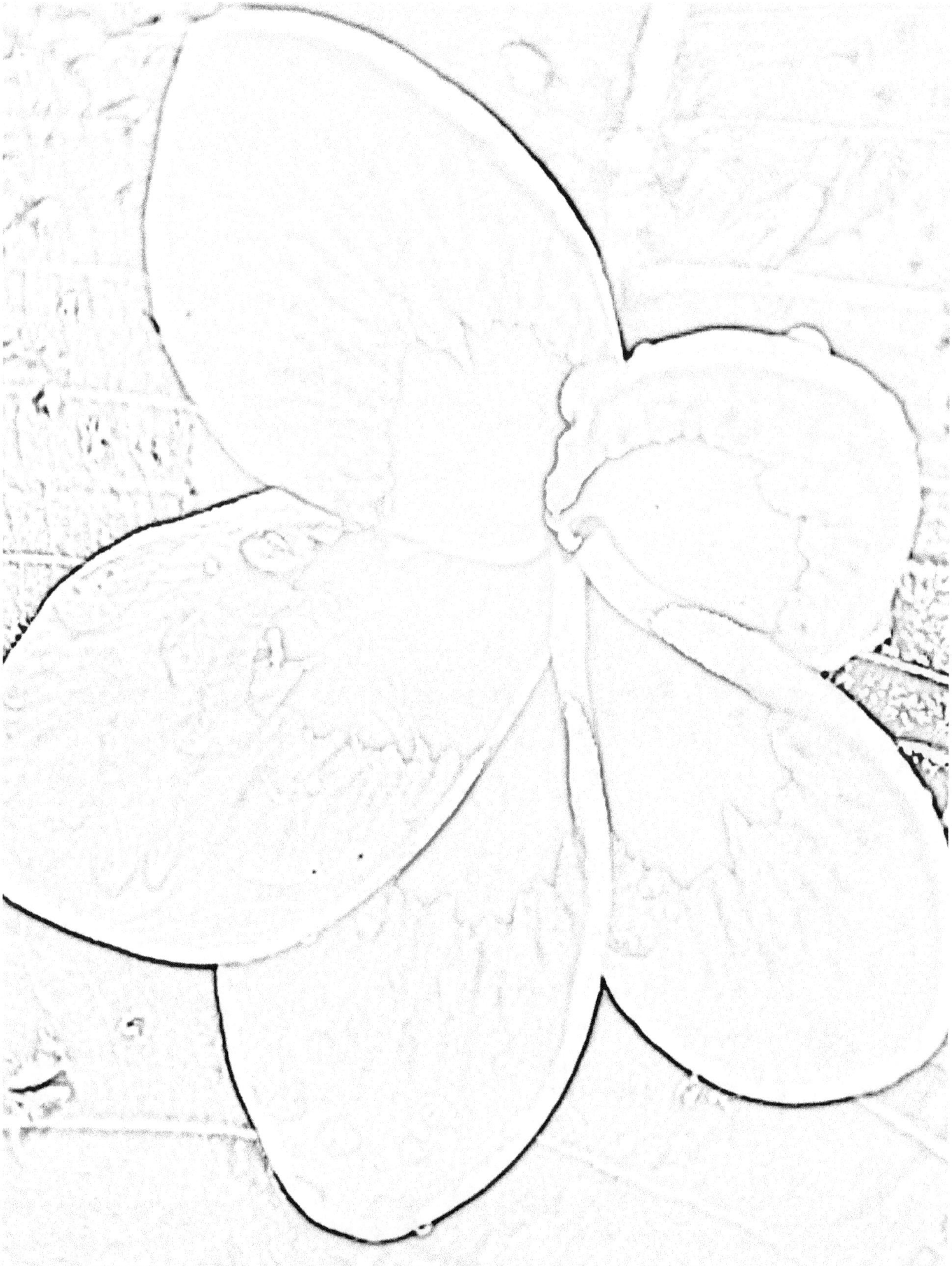

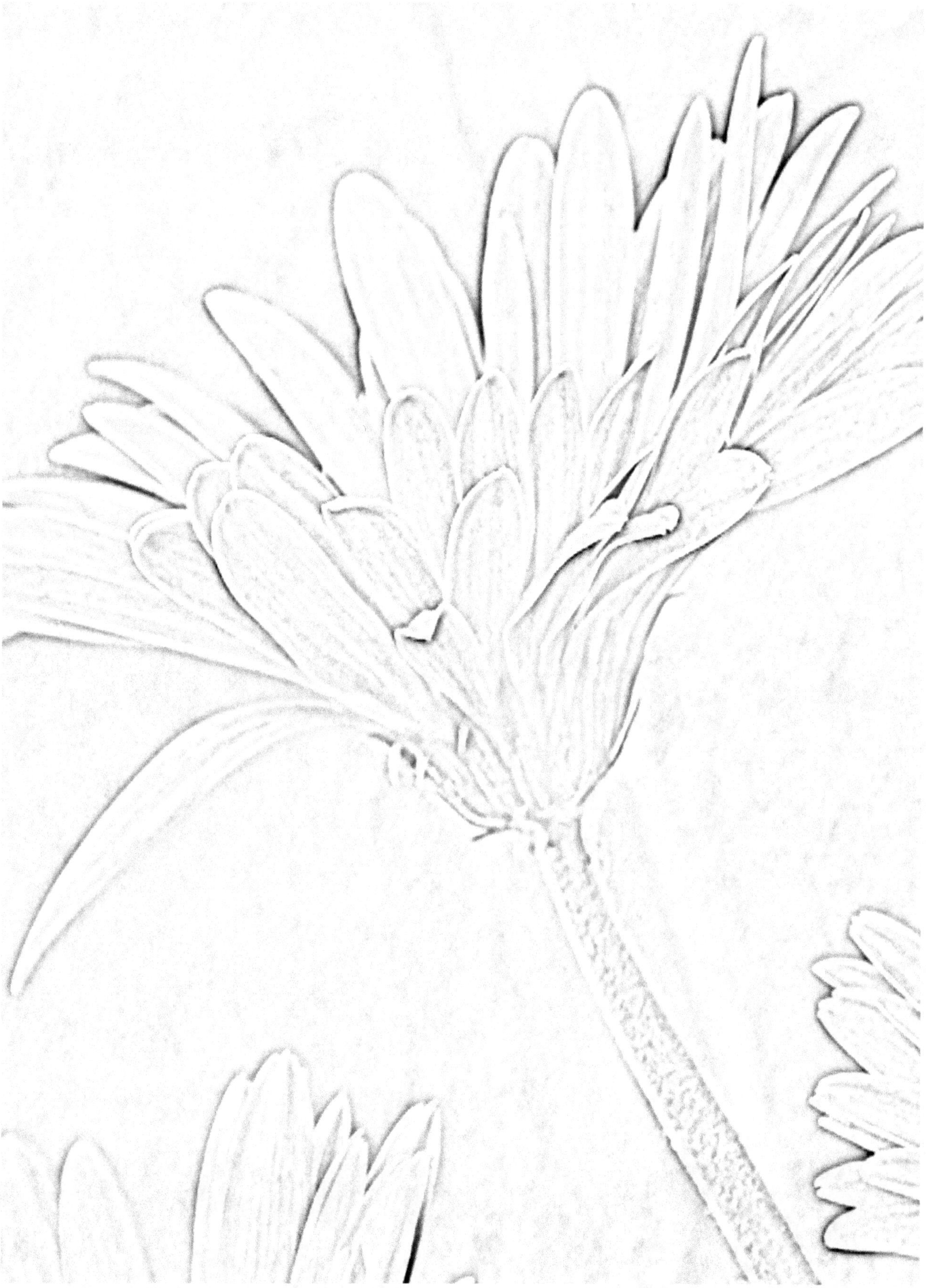

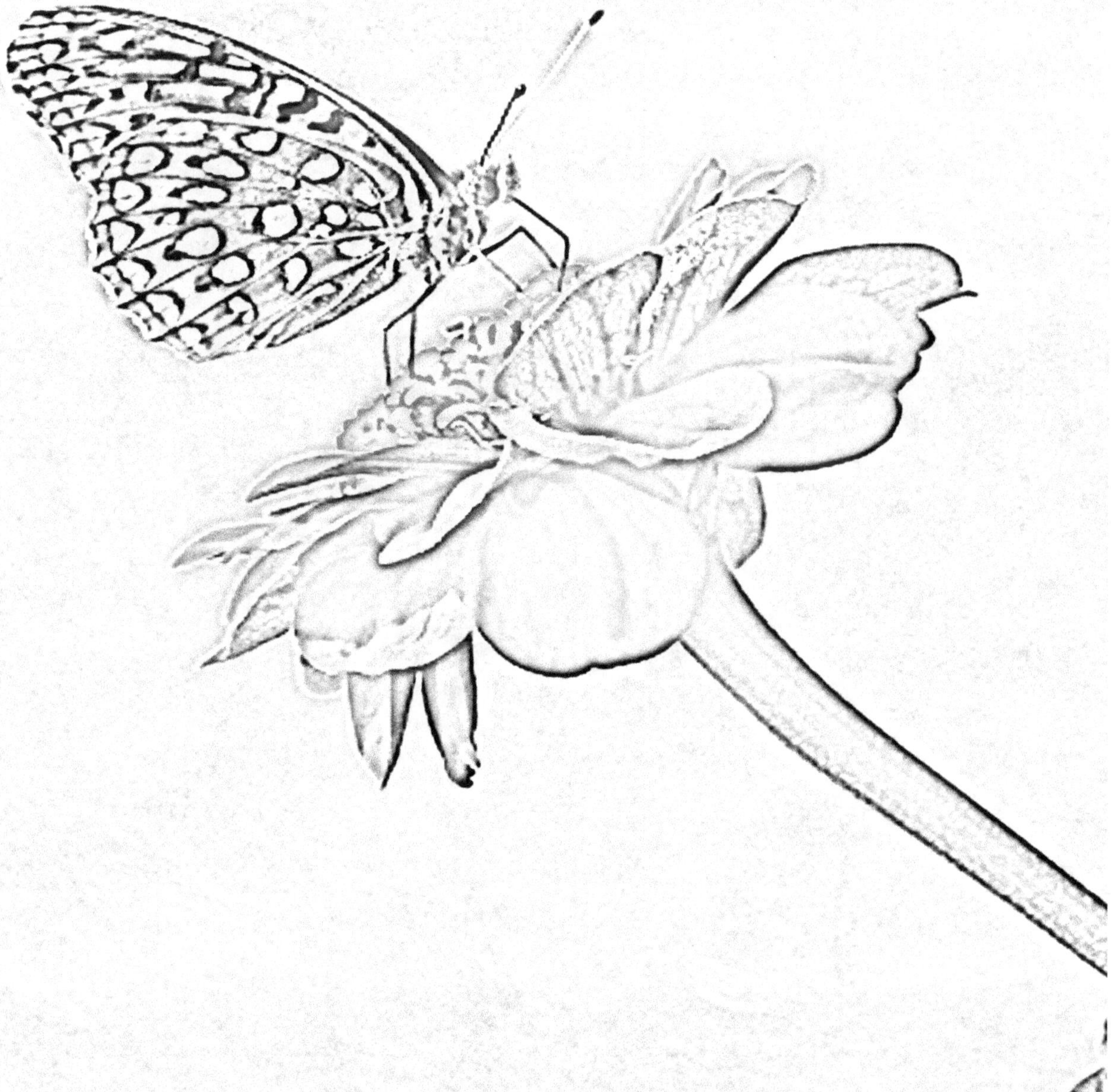

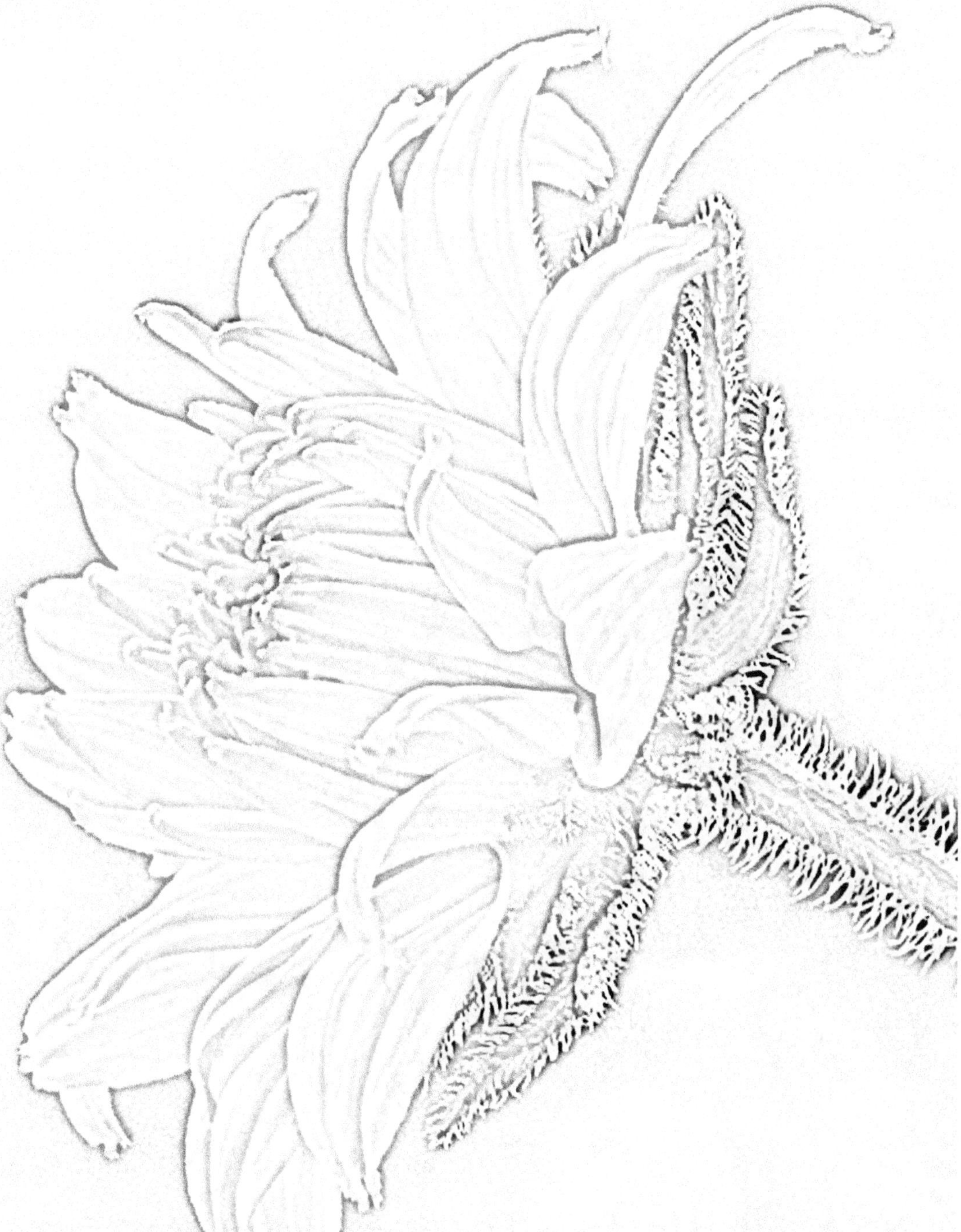

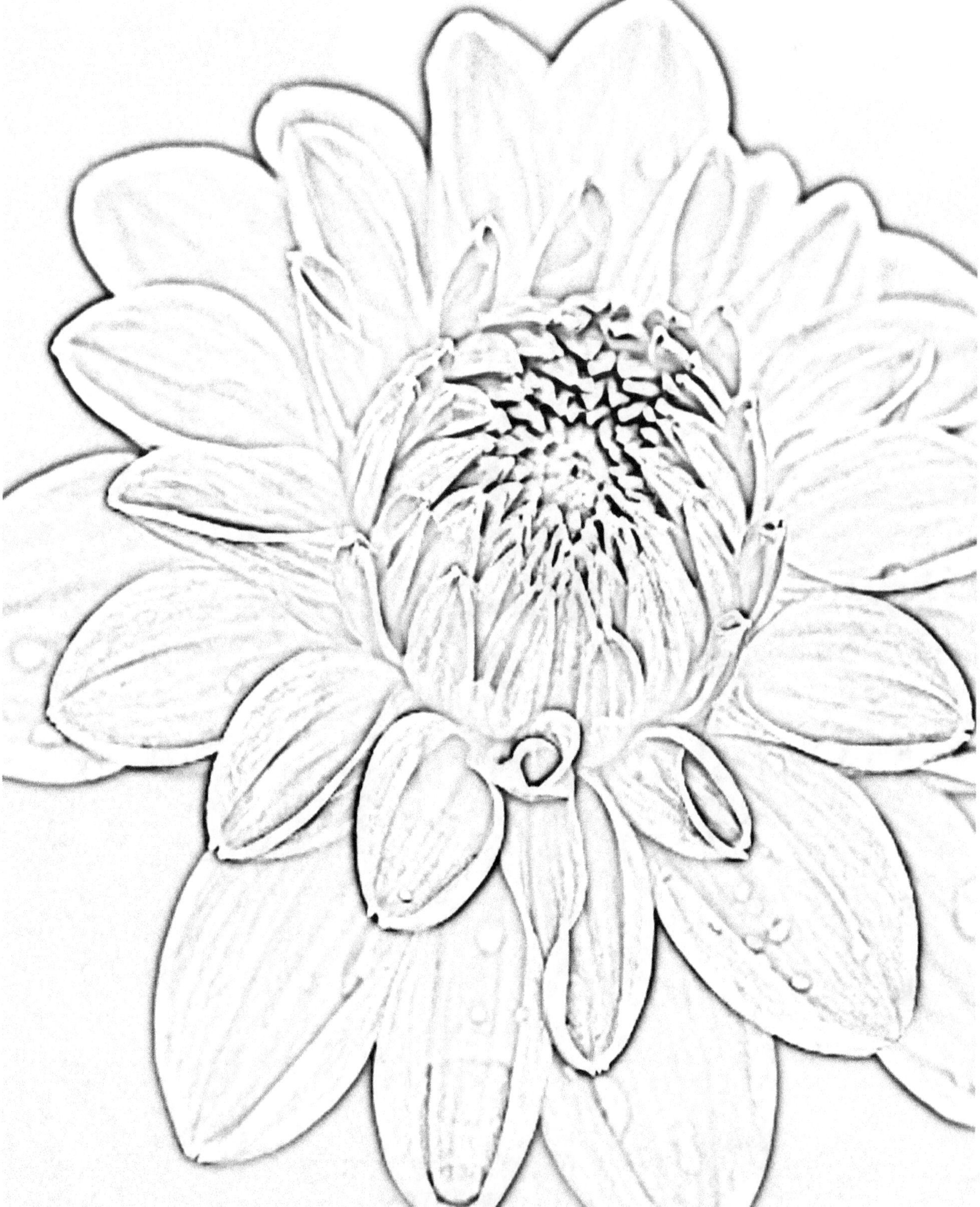

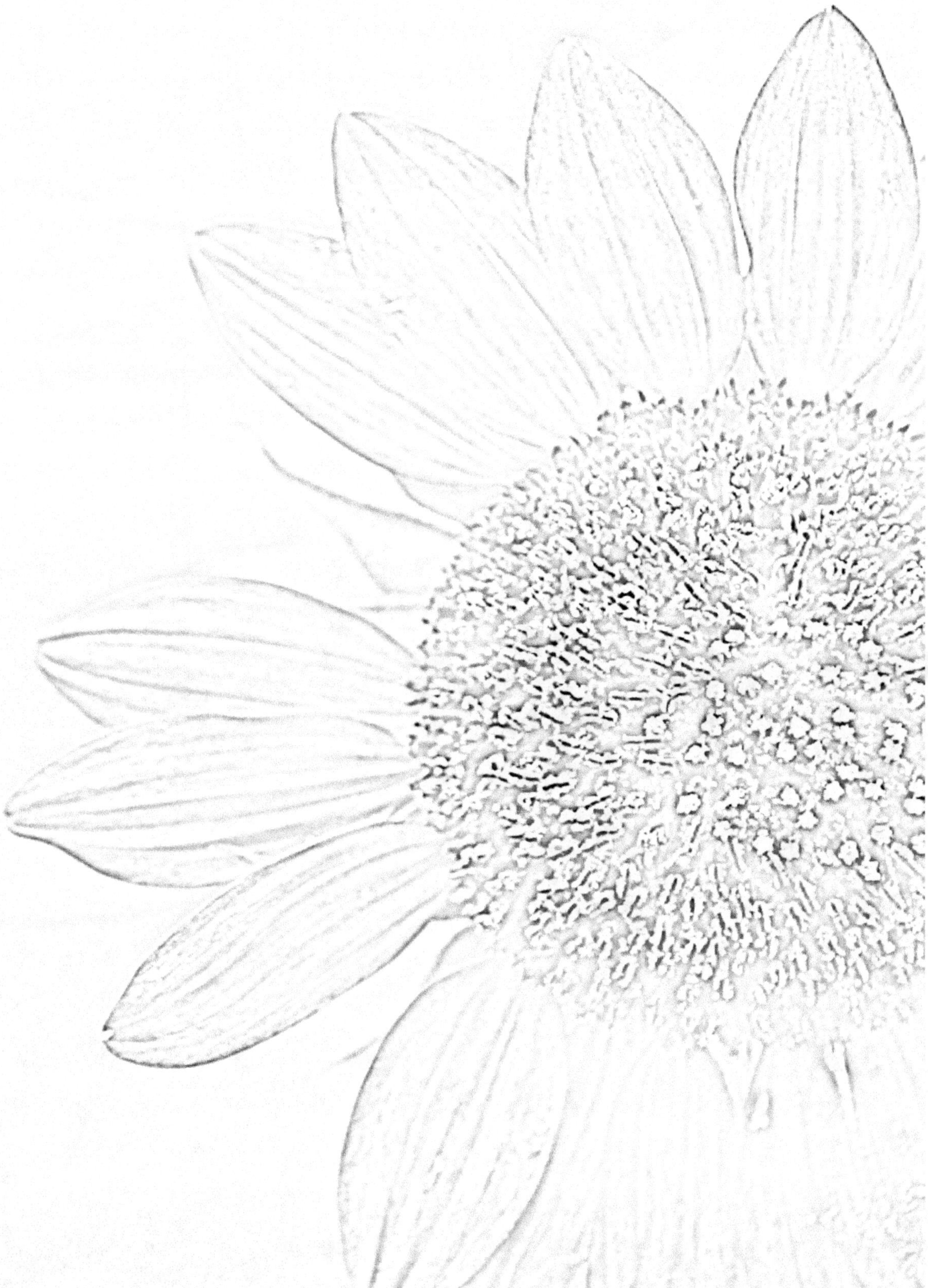

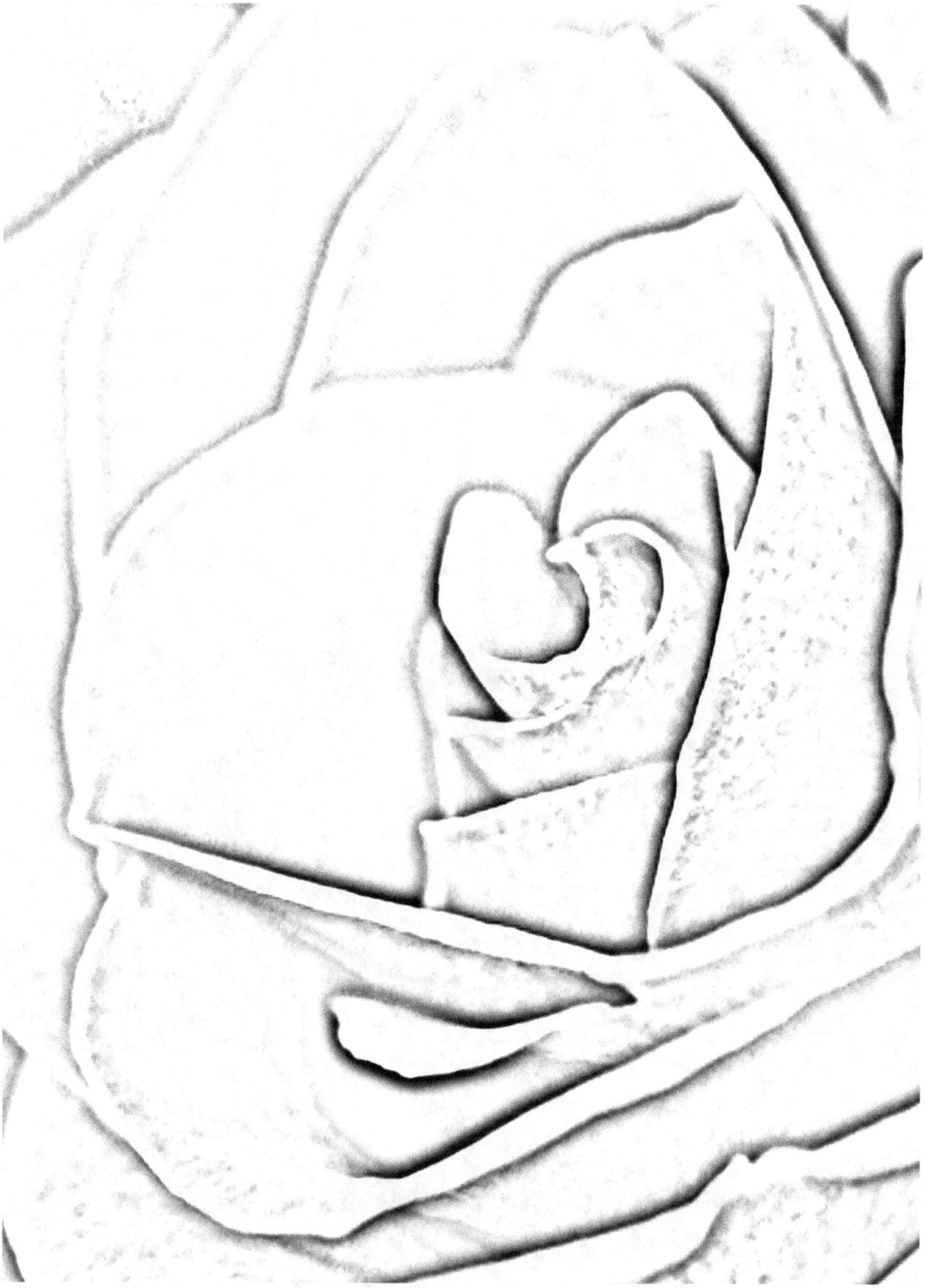

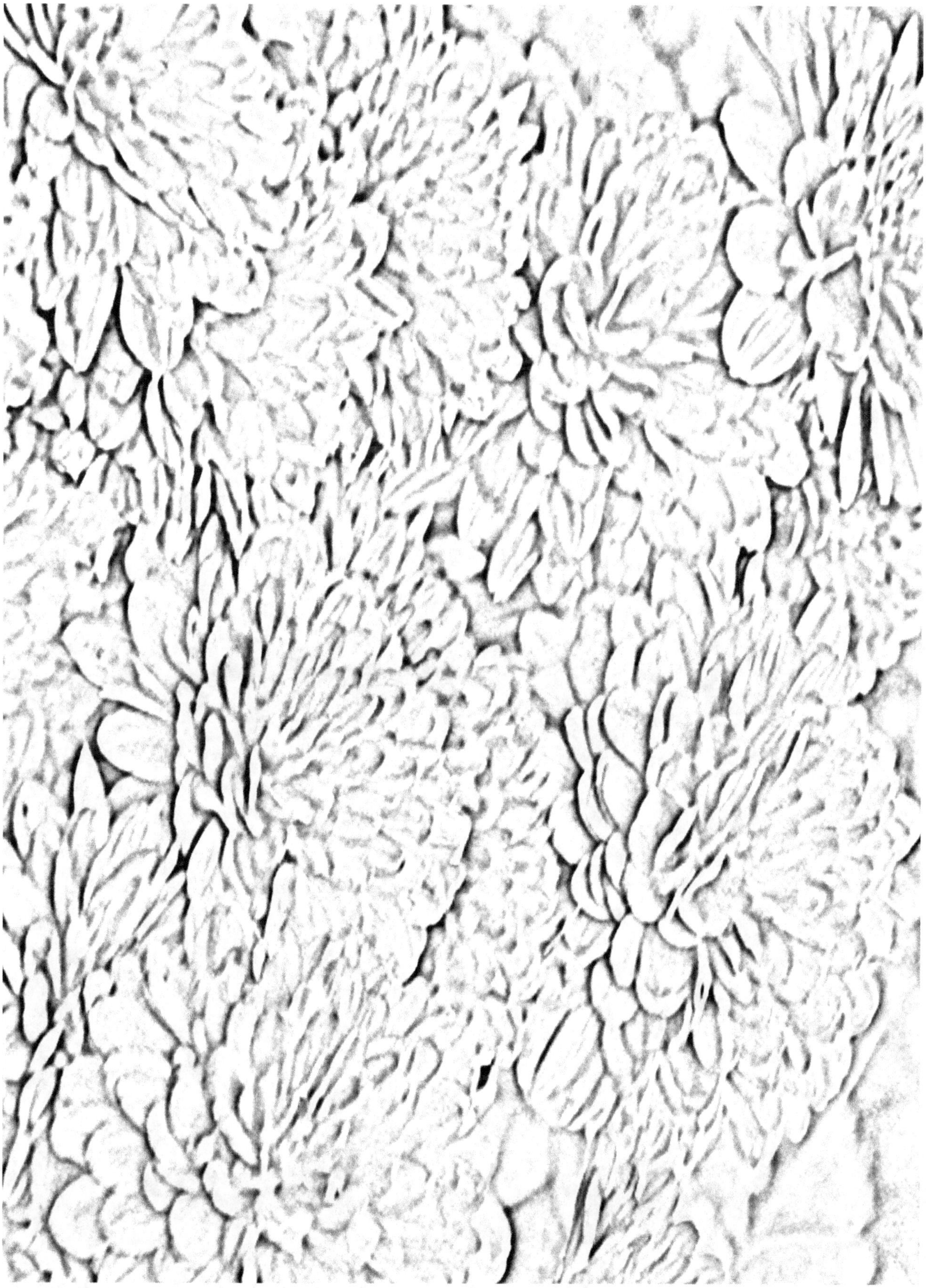

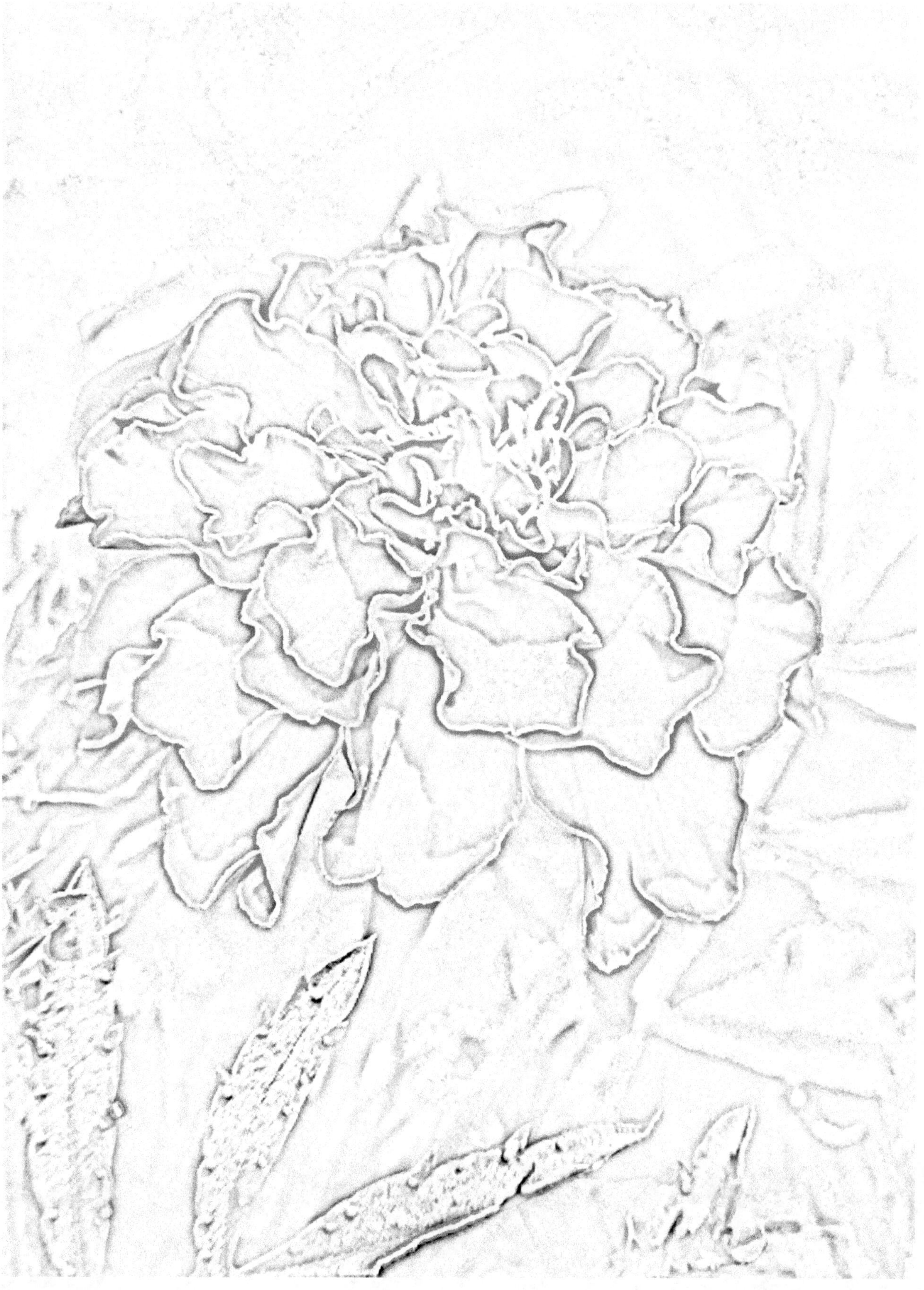

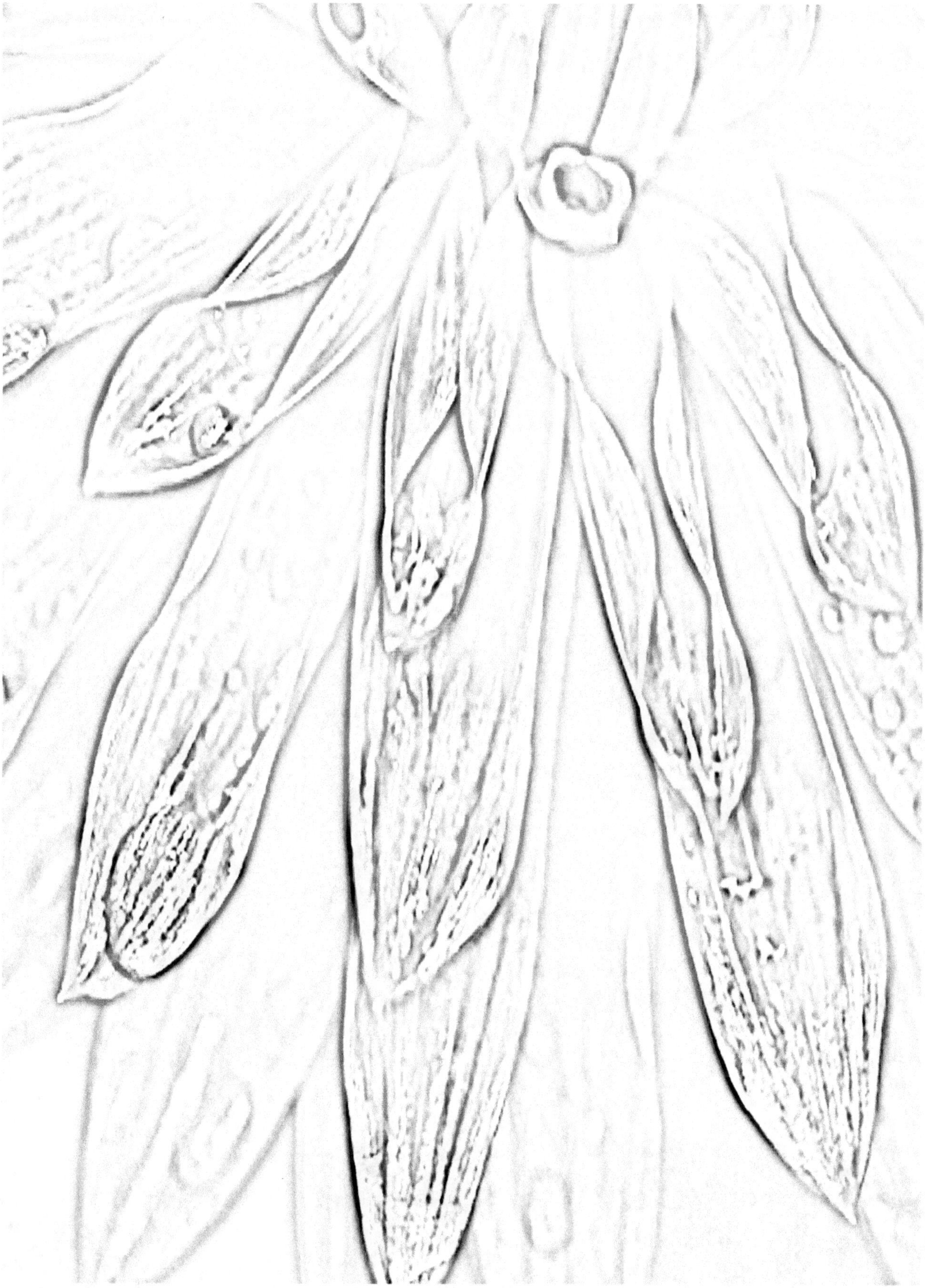

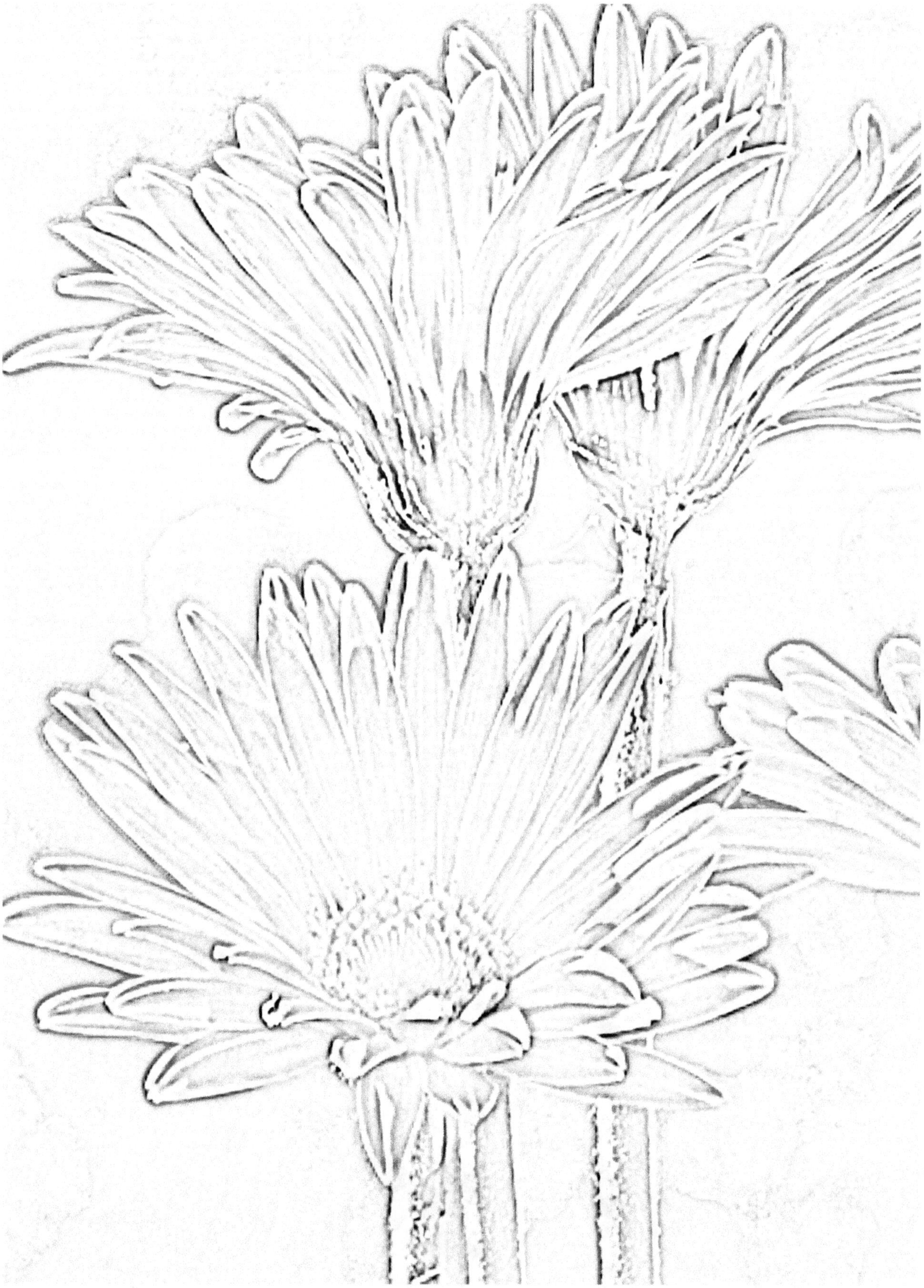

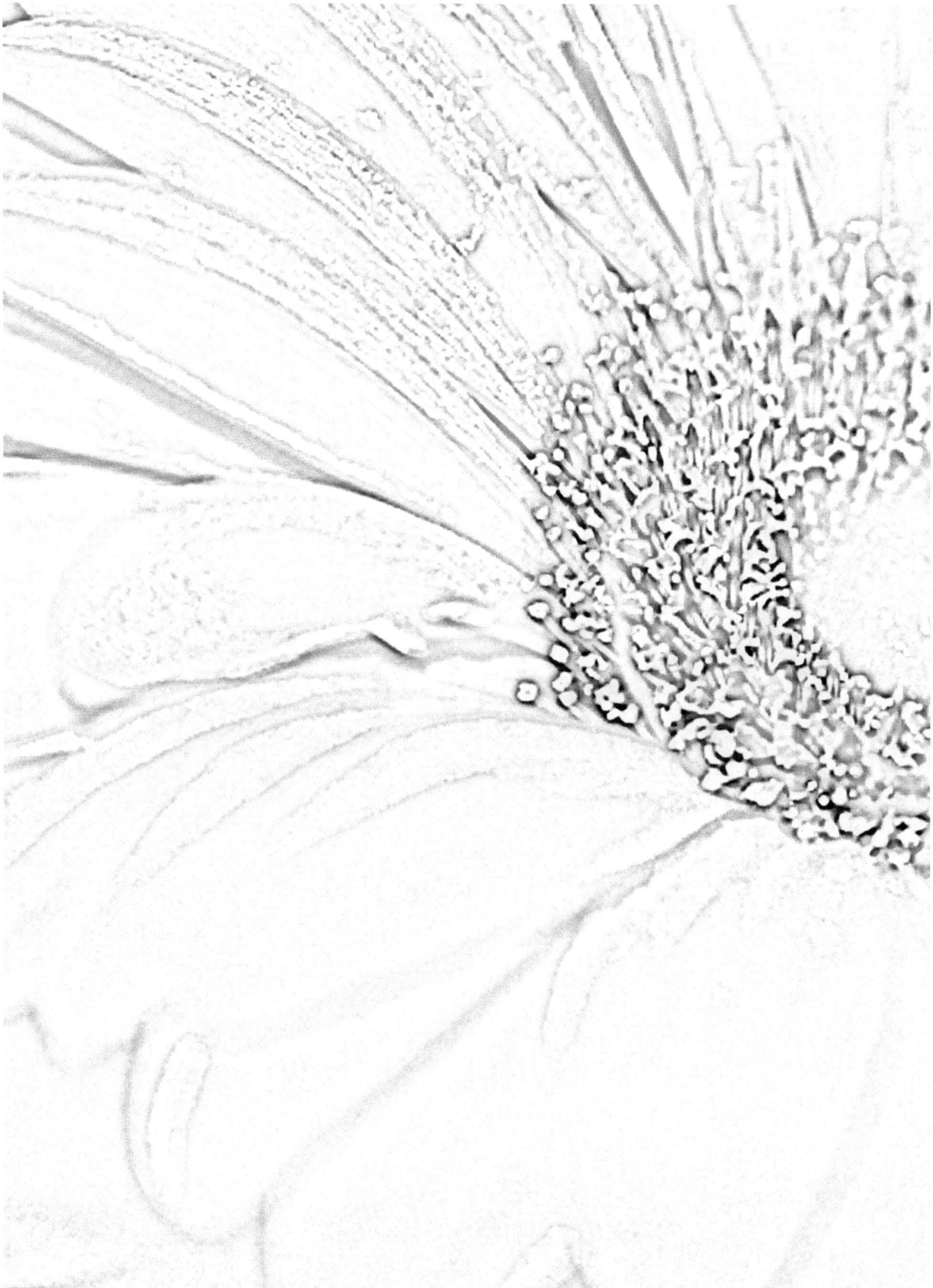

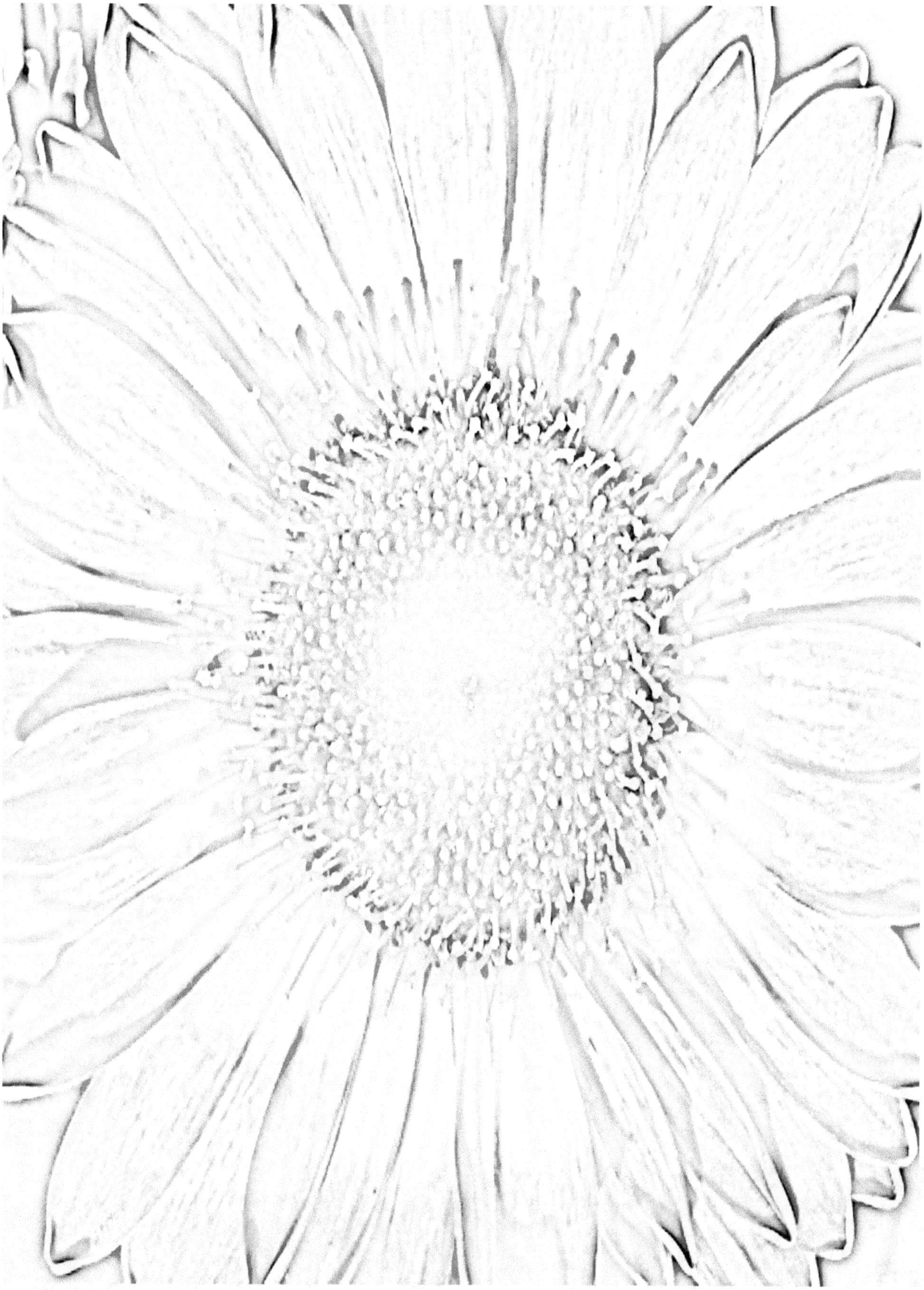

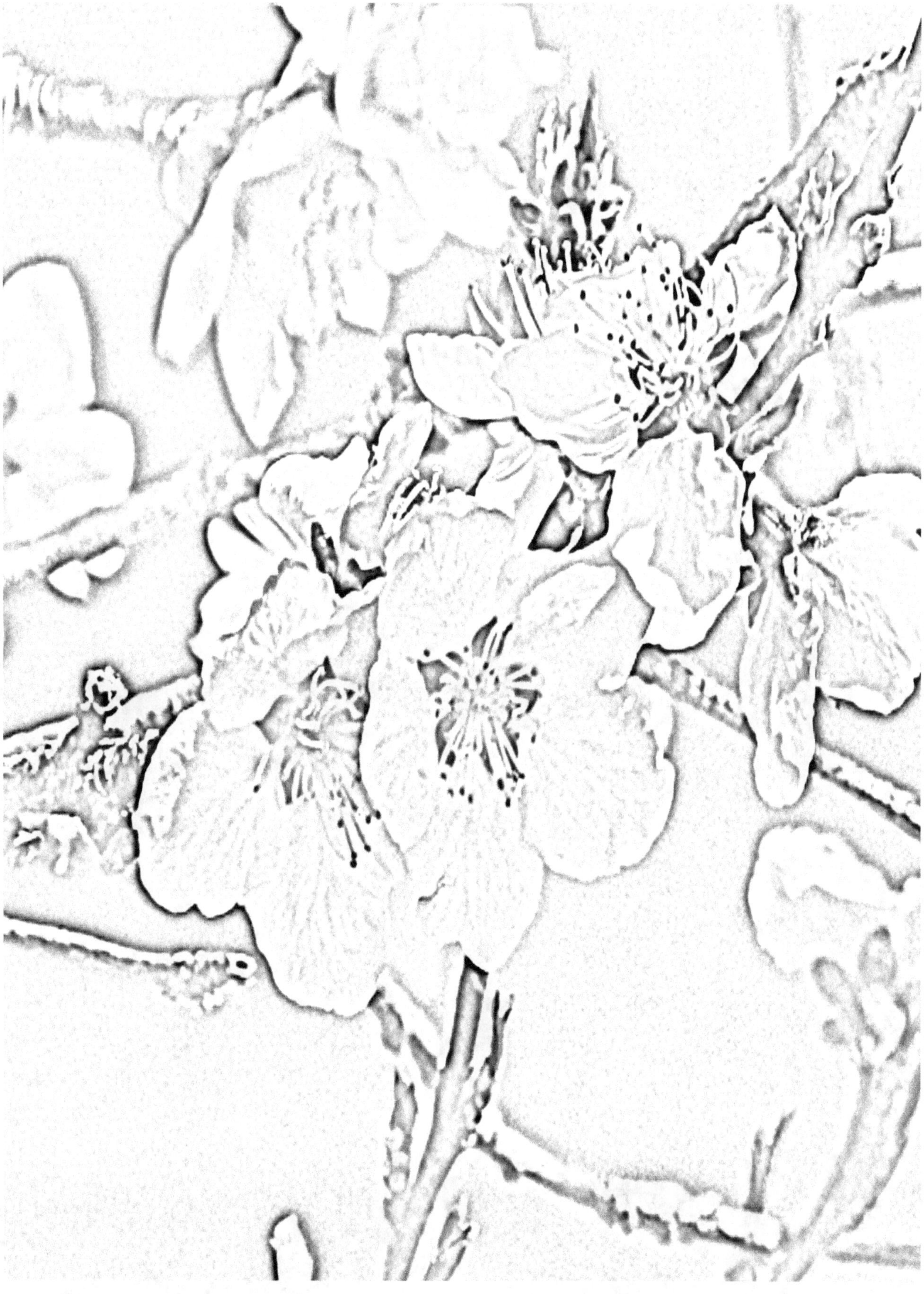

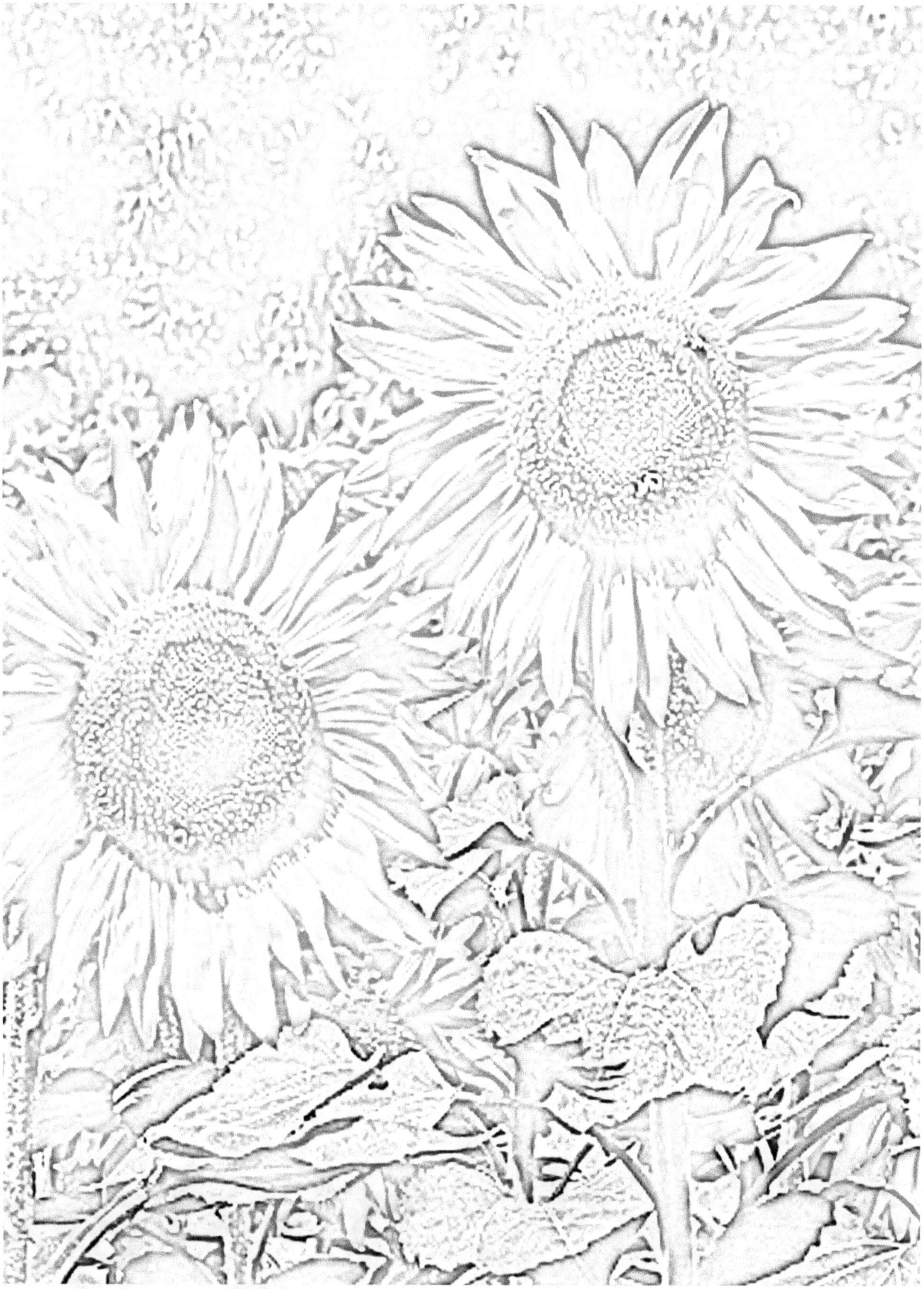

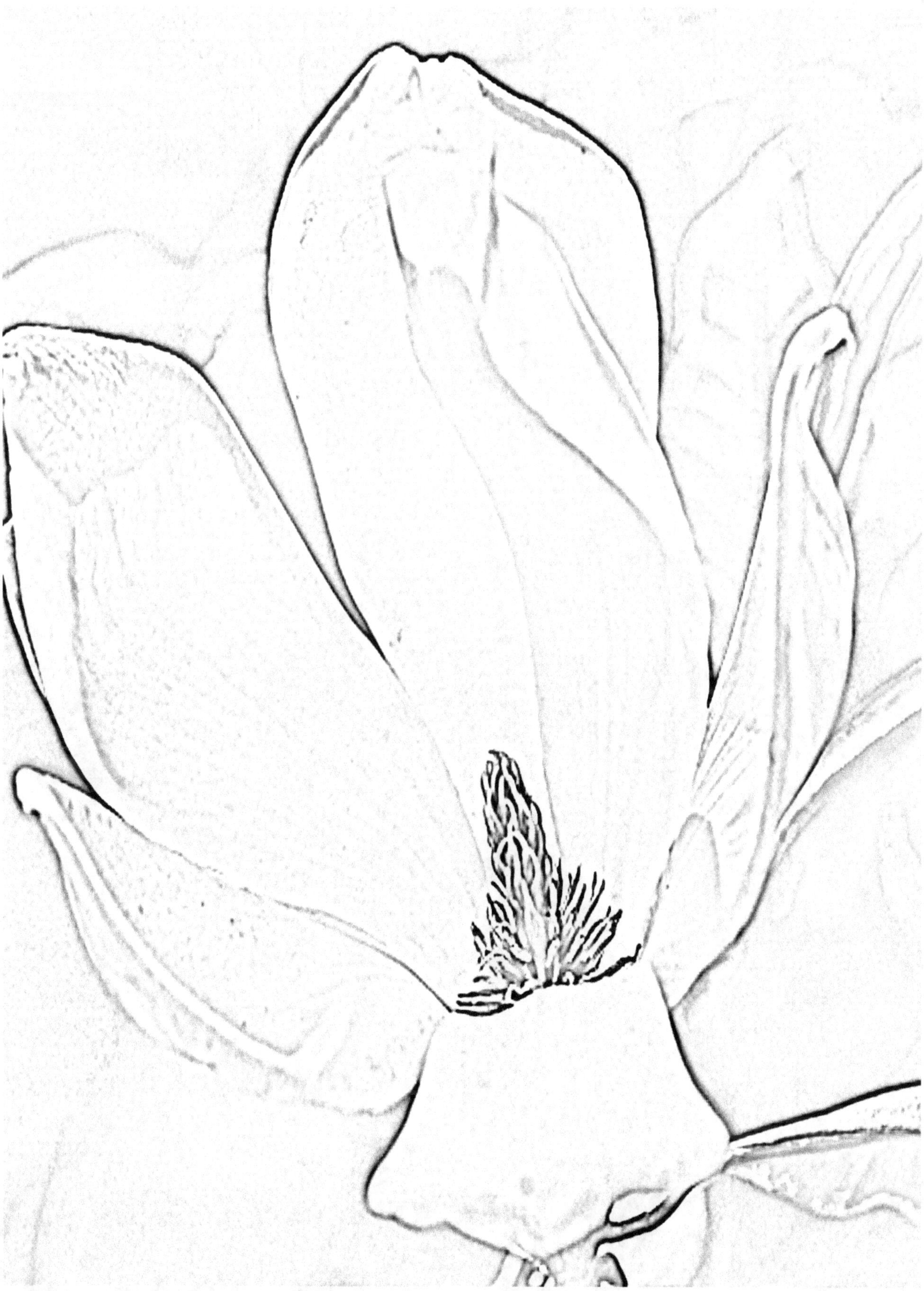

www.ingramcontent.com/pod-product-compliance
Lightning Source LLC
Chambersburg PA
CBHW081404170526
45166CB00010B/3202
* 9 7 8 1 5 1 9 4 2 2 9 2 7 *